明陵今照

中石题

摄影/文 周元庆

明十三陵，安葬着大明王朝13位皇帝和23位皇后。自明成祖朱棣营建第一座陵墓——长陵距今已近600年；明最后一朝皇帝崇祯的思陵也已350余年。

站在蟒山之巅的"天池"——即我工作的北京十三陵蓄能电厂之"上池"——俯瞰陵区，不禁赞叹这块朱棣皇帝为他和子孙们选择的万年吉地。明永乐五年（公元1407年），明成祖朱棣命礼部尚书赵羾率风水术士在北京郊区卜选陵地。至天寿山（原名黄土山），见龙盘虎踞，盆地平川，一泻千里，极具帝王之气，便按照明朝的规制，将这大约40平方千米的洞天福地，辟为建造帝王陵寝之地。

公元1540年（明嘉靖十九年），在虎山把守的入口处，建起一座石牌坊，并派护军把守，从此这里成为皇家禁地，无人再敢虎视鹰瞵。

史料记载：天寿山"山崇高正大、雄伟宽宏"、"昆仑以来之北干王气所聚矣。内则蟒山盘其左，虎峪距其右，凤凰翥其南，黄花城、四海冶拥其后；外则西有西山、东有马兰峪，群峰罗列如几如屏、如拱如抱、如万骑簇拥、如千官侍从。"

十三陵的建筑是我国风水理论的典型代表，堪称一部旷世的杰作，"峰峦矗拥、众水环绕……依山面水"，"叠嶂层层献奇于后，龙脉抱卫，砂水翕聚……山川之灵秀、造化之精英凝结融会于其中"。正如英国著名科学史家李约瑟所说，皇陵在中国建筑形制上是一个重大的成就……它整个图案的内容也许就是整个建筑部分与风景艺术相结合的最伟大的例子。

在近600年的历史中，十三陵饱经沧桑。她经历了兵燹与天灾的破坏；数百年风霜雨雪的侵蚀，更使当年巍峨壮观、金碧辉煌的帝陵失去些许风采。然而唯其如此，却愈发使人在厚重的历史面前久久地凝望、久久地沉吟。

2006年1月，承蒙十三陵特区领导的批准，我得以对十三陵陵区进行全方位拍摄，包括进入封闭管理、尚未开放的陵墓。在一年的时间里，每次端着相机走进陵区的时候，我都怀着对中华传统文化的虔诚、敬仰、自豪和慨叹的心情，而这种心情都凝聚在我的每一幅照片中。

沿神道进入安葬成祖朱棣的长陵，我领略了帝陵的恢宏；而顺着崎岖的村间小路来到崇祯帝朱由检的思陵时，比普通百姓的坟包大不了多少的宝顶、残存粗糙的祾恩殿砖石，在我面前组成了"亡国之君"四个大字。在已列入计划但尚未进行修缮的英宗朱祁镇的裕陵、宪宗朱见深的茂陵，原汁原味的残陵景象勾人顿发思古之幽情。在这两座陵里我投入了极大的精力；因为，一年后，面前的一切都将不再。

我想，您翻阅这本画册，一定会觉得这些摄入镜头的画面比记忆或现实中的十三陵更美妙；您带着这本图册到十三陵按图索骥，也会感到您自己眼中的美景胜过我镜头中的图画。这是因为明陵的景致与文化底蕴是没有边际的，是永远奥妙无穷的，永远在等待着后人的发现、认识和醒悟——所以她才会成为举世闻名的永恒的历史文化遗产。

联合国世界遗产组织第27届大会已将明十三陵列入《世界遗产名录》。作为一名摄影人，能够通过我的镜头把陵区（尤其是世人不甚了解、无法看到的陵墓）的画面展献给人们，我感到非常的欣慰。

深深感谢我国著名教育家、书法家欧阳中石先生为本书题写书名；

感谢十三陵特区的鼎立协助，为我的拍摄提供便利；

感谢华北电网有限公司、北京十三陵蓄能电厂给予我的培养与扶持。

Ming Tombs, comprised of the mausoleums of 13 emperors and 23 empresses of Ming Dynasty, have a history of 600 years since the first mausoleum of Chengzu Zhu Di was built. It's more than 350 years since the last emperor Chongzhen was buried in Si Ling.

Overlooking the Ming Tombs area from the top of the Mangshan Mountain, where the "Pool of Heaven" is located, (it's also the upper reservoir of Shisanling (Ming Tombs) Pumped Storage Power Station where I am working at), I can't help admiring this eternal and fortunate ground that was selected by emperor Zhu Di for himself and his offsprings. In the 5th year of Yongle (1407 A.D.), along with several Fengshui masters, Zhaohong, the minister of the Board of Rites, was assigned by Chengzu Zhu Di to choose the site for his mausoleum around Beijing. When they came to Tianshou Mountain (formerly called Huangtu Mountain), they found that it was such a large and open area which is flat in the center and surrounded by the tiger and dragon hills sitting on both sides, symbolizing the supreme power of emperors. Finally they enclosed this auspicious ground of about 40 square kilometers around for construction of the emperor's mausoleum according to the regulation of Ming dynasty. At the entrance to the mausoleum where the tiger hill stands as a guard, a archway was built in 1504 A.D. (the 19th year of Jiajing) by the order of Emperor Zhu Houcong. From then on, this ground became a forbidden place with soldiers guarding around day and night and no one would dear to offend it.

It's known from historical resources that the Tianshou Mountain, grand and huge, is the north part of the Kunlun Mountain, which looks like the spirit of the supreme emperor. In the encircled basin of Tianshou, Mangshan Mountain sits on the left, the Tiger Hill on the right and Fenghuang Mountain at its south. While Huanghuacheng and Sihaiye embraced it from behind. From its outside are Xishan Mountain at the west and Malanyu at the east. A number of hills and mountains circle around like the emperor's officials and guards.

The architecture of Ming Tombs is the significant example of the Chinese principles of geomancy (fengshui), and also a masterpiece across centuries. Just like what the famous British scientist Joseph Li described in his book, the architecture style and the mausoleum layouts of the Ming Tombs were great accomplishments, and the complete plan was the greatest example of combination of its architecture and the landscape.

Over six hundred years of history, Ming Tombs went through difficulties and hardships, including destruction of wars and natural disasters. It is not as resplendent or magnificent as be before after hundreds of years of wearing away by power of nature. However, people like to pore over it and are deeply touched by the massive history when visiting any of the mausoleums.

In January 2006, I was very glad to be approved by the heads of Ming Tombs Special District to take pictures in every corner of the mausoleums, including those which are not open to the public. Each time when I came into the mausoleum, a mixed feelings of admiration, pride and regret to the great traditional Chinese culture rush into my heart and all my feelings have been condensed in each of my pictures.

Along the Sacred Road, I came into Chang Ling where Chengzu Zhu Di was buried. I appreciated the significance of the mausoleum. However, when I came across the zigzagged country road and stood in front of Si Ling where the last emperor Zhu Youjian was buried, looking over the tomb which is not that bigger than a common person and watching the remained raspy bricks of the existing Ling'en Hall, I can't help sighing the circumstance of the emperor of a conquered nation.

I was also devoted to the Yu Ling where Zhu Qizhen was buried and Mao Ling where Zhu Jianshen slept since the two mausoleums were on the maintenance list in the near future. The original appearances of the incomplete mausoleums are more attractive because of their ancient taste and deep historic meanings. However, everything will not be the same anymore after a year.

When you read this photographic album, you may feel that the pictures of Ming Tombs are far more splendid than that in your memory or reality. If you visit the Ming Tombs by following up the clues in this album, you may find that the beautiful scenes are even more magnificent than the photos. All the possibility is reasonable because the scenic splendors and cultural connotation inside the Ming Tombs is never ended. Its profundity is to be recognized by later generations. That is why the Ming Tombs is taken as the world famous historical and cultural heritage.

The Ming Tombs were listed in the World Heritage Record in the 27th anniversary of the World Heritage Organization of the United Nation. Being a photographer, I was very grateful to have this opportunity to show the mausoleums to the public through my lens, in particular those which are unfamiliar or unknown.

On this occasion, I would like to deeply appreciate Mr. Ouyang Zhongshi, the famous Chinese educator and calligrapher, for inscribing the title for this album.

I would also thank Ming Tombs Special District for providing convenience of taking photos for me, North China Grid Company Limited and Shisanling (Ming Tombs) Pumped Storage Power Plant for great support and help to me.

十三陵各陵的陵前都有一条神道。其中长陵的神道最长，亦称总神道，约为7.3公里。神道的墓仪设施种类和数量也最多，显示出了十三陵中祖陵的尊崇地位和宏大气势。

　　神道最南端是一座高大的石牌坊，建于明嘉靖十九年（1540年），为仿木结构。它是我国营建时间最早的高等级石牌坊，雕刻非常精美。神道两侧分列着石兽石人，古称"石像生"。石人排在石兽之后，均为站立形象。这些石像生体量高大，造型设计端庄威猛，具有明显的写实风格，与肃穆庄严的陵寝建筑和谐统一，并从意向上起到"保护墓葬，趋吉避凶"的作用，达到了非常高的艺术境界。

　　十三陵的建筑均为红色墙面、黄色琉璃瓦顶，这是体现中国古代礼制所规定的尊卑等级秩序。《周礼》提出了"尚赤"的礼制思想；遵此，明朝的宫殿、陵寝墙面都采用红色。

　　明朝建造皇宫与陵寝时，深受易学文化影响。"古之王者择天下之中而立国，择国之中而立宫。"按五行之色，东方为木，其色青；南方为火，其色红；西方为金，其色白；北方为水，其色黑；中央为土，其色黄。天子之宫既然处"居中而尊"的位置，就必然采用黄色为屋顶颜色。

Each mausoleum of the Ming Tombs has a Sacred Road. The one of Chang Ling with the most diverse monuments and statuaries is the longest, with the length of 7.3 kilometers. It is also the reflection of the supreme status and grandiosity of the ancestral mausoleum.

There stands a huge stone archway at the southern end of the Sacred Road. Built in the 9th year of Jiajing (1540 A.D.), it is the earliest large ceremonial archway in China and is also a masterpiece of carving. The archway appears to be timberwork even though it is actually made of stone. On both sides of the Sacred Road, there are stone animals and human statues. The stone human statues standing behind the stone animals, full of power and grandeur, tall and grand, are masterpieces of arts. With realistic style, they are integrated with the solemn mausoleum and in function of protection.

The architectures of the Ming Tombs have the unified characters of red wall and yellow glazed-bricked roof, which indicate the idea of the grade order of distinguishing the supreme and the lower ranks according to the ancient custom and rites. From the Confucian ethnic idea, red is the most honored color for the emperor therefore it was used for painting of the metope for all of the palaces and mausoleums in Ming dynasty.

The culture of Book of Changes deeply affects the construction of the imperial palace and mausoleum in Ming dynasty. For example, the Book says the ancient emperors always chose the central point under the sun to establish their kingdom and built their palaces at the central point of the kingdom. According to the Chinese wuxing theory, east stands for wood with the color of green; north stands for fire with the color of red; west stands for gold with the color of white; north stands for water with the color of black, while the center stands for soil with the color of yellow. That is why yellow was grandly used for the roof of imperial palaces.

神道 The Sacred Road

陵门　永陵　The Entrance Gate, Yongling

↑陵门　长陵　　The Entrance Gate，Changling

→祾恩门　德陵　　The Ling'en Gate，Deling

↑ 祾恩门遗址　庆陵　Ruins of the Ling'en Gate, Qingling

← 祾恩门遗址　景陵　Ruins of the Ling'en Gate, Jingling

世界文化遗产
WORLD CULTURAL HERITAGE
明十三陵－康陵
THE MING TOMBS KANGLING

红墙 康陵
The Red Wall, Kangling

红墙 献陵

The Red Wall, Xianling

红墙 永陵

The Red Wall, Yongling

红墙 长陵
The Red Wall, Changling

红墙 永陵
The Red Wall, Yongling

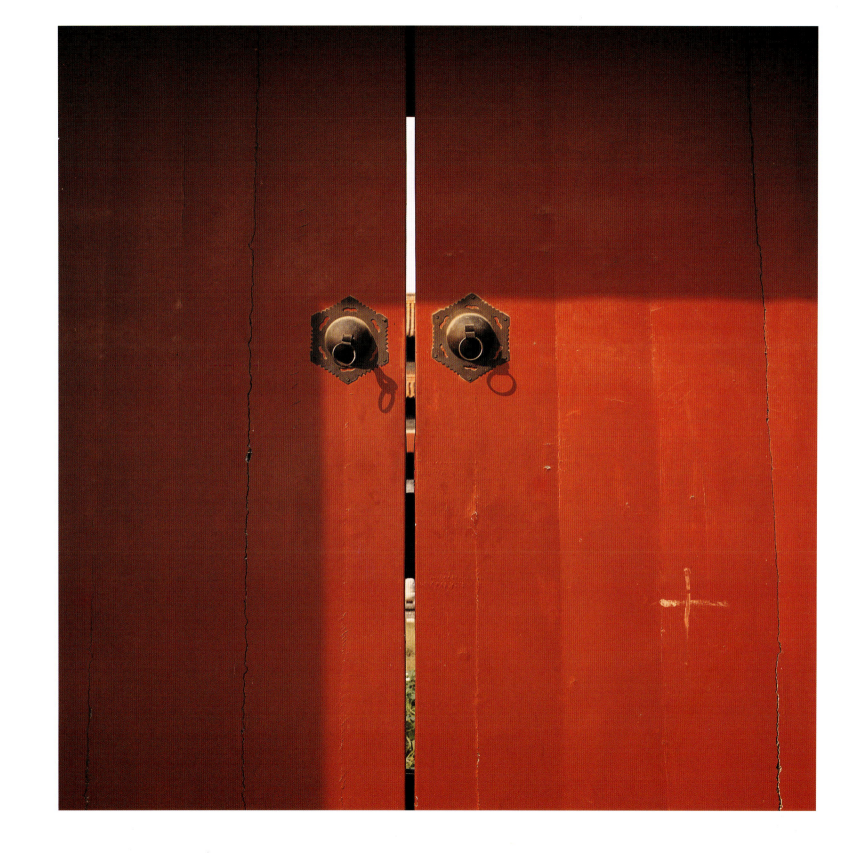

红门 庆陵
The Red Door, Qingling

华表　神道

The Marble pillar
at the Sacred Road

石像生　神道

The Stone Animals and Officials at the Sacred Road

宝城内景 康陵　Scenery inside the Treasure City, Kangling

宝城内月牙墙 昭陵　The Crescent Wall inside the Treasure City, Zhaoling

石券门　茂陵

The Stone Shrine Gate，Maoling

永陵　Yongling　　　　　茂陵　Maoling　　　　　茂陵　Maoling

马道　永陵

The Bridle Road, Yongling

方城月台礓嚓道　茂陵

Qiangca Ramp, Maoling

马道 裕陵
The Bridle Road，Yuling

马道 茂陵
The Bridle Road，Maoling

马道 裕陵
The Bridle Road，Yuling

明楼　献陵

The Memorial Shrine,
Xianling

明楼 永陵

The Memorial Shrine, Yongling

明楼 康陵

The Memorial Shrine, Kangling

明楼　茂陵

The Memorial Shrine, Maoling

明楼　裕陵

The Memorial Shrine,
Yuling

圣号碑　定陵
The Divine Merit
Stele, Dingling

圣号碑　庆陵

The Divine Merit Stele, Qingling

圣号碑　永陵

The Divine Merit Stele, Yongling

残明楼　茂陵

The Relic Memorial Shine, Maoling

明楼　庆陵
The Memorial Shrine,
Qingling

方城侧面石台阶　永陵

The Stone Stairs beside
the Square City, Yongling

宝城内转向礓嚓道　德陵

Qiangca Ramp, Deling

哑巴院内排水孔 昭陵
The Waterspout in the Yabayuan
(Isolated Yard Facing the Tomb), Zhaoling

隧道门 定陵
The Tunnel Gate, Dingling

宝城墙砌砖　永陵
The Bricks of the
City Wall, Yongling

马道　定陵
The Bridle Road,
Dingling

马道　献陵

The Bridle Road, Xianling

宝城墙　德陵

The Outside Wall of the Treasure City, Deling

影壁　德陵
The Screen Wall, Deling

影壁　茂陵
The Screen Wall, Maoling

影壁 德陵
The Screen Wall,
Deling

明朝时，陵区内外及神道两侧都种植了大量的树木，"大红门以内苍松翠柏数十万株"，到清初始被伐尽。但各陵陵宫内仍然松柏参天，郁郁葱葱。几百年过去，这些古树也已成为一道吸引游客的景观。而且，有些滋生的树木在建筑物上扎根、成长、壮大，不禁让人感叹这些树木顽强的生命力。

　　在安葬明朝最后一个皇帝朱由检（崇祯帝）的思陵，有一个奇特的景观－断头松。几株松树的上半部像被刀砍掉一样，余下的树干造型，似乎很痛苦地扭曲着、呼号着。每有游人至此，无不称奇感叹。

According to the history book, there were tens of thousands of pine trees and cypresses planted inside the Great Red Gate, as well as the mausoleum area and both sides of the Sacred Road. At the beginning of Qing Dynasty, lots of the trees were cut down except those inside the mausoleum that were flourishingly growing until now. They even became one of the sightseeing points that attract the tourists after several hundreds of years. More amazingly, some of the trees took roots and flourishingly grew along the buildings, which shows their extremely strong lift force.

At the Si Ling where Zhu Youjian (also called Chongzhen)—the last emperor of Ming dynasty was buried, there is a vagarious sight called the decollation pine trees, just as their name implies, the top of the trees are chopped off while the stems are distorted as if they were mooing.

古树　永陵　The Ancient Trees, Yongling

古树　裕陵　The Ancient Trees, Yuling

古树　景陵　The Ancient Trees, Jingling

古树　景陵

The Ancient Trees,

Jingling

古树　景陵
The Ancient Trees，Jingling

古树　永陵
The Ancient Trees，Yongling

古树　永陵
The Ancient Trees，Yongling

古树　德陵
The Ancient Trees, Deling

古树　永陵
The Ancient Trees, Yongling

鹿角柏 定陵
The Buckhorn Cypress,
Dingling

断头松　思陵

The Decollation Pine

Trees, Siling

断头松　思陵

The Decollation Pine Trees, Siling

明朝对陵区的保卫、保护非常重视，划定了陵寝禁山范围。凡在陵区剪伐树木、取土取石、开窑烧造、放火烧山者，主犯处极刑，从者发边卫充军。为此，设立了陵寝军事保卫组织，还营建了供太监居住的神宫监。目前，德陵的神宫监还基本保持着外围原貌，村民们在此平静祥和地生活着。

The security of the mausoleum is very important in Ming Dynasty. A forbidden area was enclosed around the Ming Tombs. Anyone who cut trees, took the earth and stones, opened a brick stove or lit fire inside the forbidden area, would be executed and the accessory would be exiled.

Therefore, military security organization was developed and Shengongjian was built for the eunuchs to live. At present, the appearance of the Shengongjian is still conserved and the descendants of the security army live a quiet and auspicious life there.

神宫监 德陵 The Shengongjian, Deling

民居 德陵神宫监　The Civilians' Residence of Shengongjian, Deling

街道　德陵神宫监

Street Scene of Shengongjian, Deling

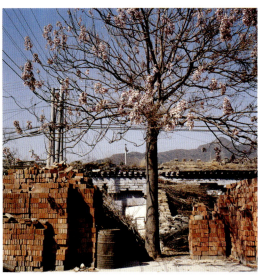

院落　德陵神宫监

Courtyard of Shengongjian, Deling

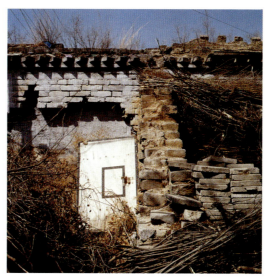

石碾 德陵神宫监
The Stone Grind in
Shengongjian, Deling

器具 德陵神宫监

Instrument in Shengongjian, Deling

民居　德陵神宫监

The Civilians' Residence of Shengongjian, Deling

民居　德陵神宫监
The Civilians' Residence
of Shengongjian, Deling

1957 年，十三陵被北京市政府定为重点古建文物保护单位；1961 年，被国务院定为全国重点文物保护单位。自 1955 年始，先后有长、永、景、定、献、昭、思、德、泰九陵得到修缮。

景、定、献、昭、思、德、泰九陵得到修缮。

In 1957, the Ming Tombs were nominated the special protection unit for ancient architecture relics by Beijing Municipal Government. In 1961, it became the National Special Protection Units of Culture Heritage. From 1955, nine of the Ming tombs which were Chang Ling, Yong Ling, Jing Ling, Ding Ling, Xian Ling, Zhao Ling, Si Ling, De Ling, Tai Ling were main—

石牌坊 长陵神道　The Stone Archway at the Sacred Road of Changling

石桥 庆陵　The Stone Bridge, Qingling

碑亭　昭陵　The Pavilion of Stele, Zhaoling

祾恩门石栏杆 长陵　The Stone Handrail of the Ling'en Gate, Changling

石桥　德陵　The Stone Bridge, Deling

地下宫殿　定陵

The Underground Palace，Dingling

定陵出土文物

The Unearthed Historical Relics of Dingling

庆陵前的公路 The Highway in front of Qingling

无字碑　庆陵
The Unlettered Stele in Qingling

王承恩墓　思陵
Wang Chengen's tomb, Siling

谥号碑　思陵
The Stele of Temple Name in Siling

十三陵俯瞰　　*A Panorama of the Ming Tombs*

长陵俯瞰

A Panorama of Chang Ling

附录：明代帝陵一览表

陵名	皇帝姓名	年号	庙号	谥号	在位年代	世系	享年	陵址
祖陵	朱百六		德祖	玄皇帝		太祖高祖	不详	江苏省盱眙县管镇乡
	朱四九		懿祖	恒皇帝		太祖曾祖	不详	
	朱初一		熙祖	裕皇帝		太祖祖父	不详	
皇陵	朱世珍		仁祖	淳皇帝		太祖父亲	64	安徽省凤阳县西南
孝陵	朱元璋	洪武	太祖	高皇帝	1368—1398		71	南京钟山南麓
长陵	朱棣	永乐	成祖	文皇帝	1402—1424	太祖四子	65	北京昌平区天寿山下
献陵	朱高炽	洪熙	仁宗	昭皇帝	1424—1425	成祖长子	48	北京昌平区天寿山黄山寺一岭下
景陵	朱瞻基	宣德	宣宗	章皇帝	1425—1435	仁宗长子	37	北京昌平区天寿山黑山下
裕陵	朱祁镇	正统 天顺	英宗	睿皇帝	1435—1449 1457—1464	宣宗长子	38	北京昌平区天寿山石门山下
景泰帝陵	朱祁钰	景泰	代宗	景皇帝	1449—1457	宣宗次子	30	北京西郊金山下
茂陵	朱见深	成化	宪宗	纯皇帝	1464—1487	英宗长子	41	北京昌平区天寿山聚宝山下
泰陵	朱祐樘	弘治	孝宗	敬皇帝	1487—1505	宪宗三子	36	北京昌平区天寿山笔架山下
显陵	朱祐杬		睿宗	献皇帝		世宗父亲	43	湖北钟祥市松林山（又名纯德山）下
康陵	朱厚照	正德	武宗	毅皇帝	1505—1521	孝宗长子	31	北京昌平区天寿山莲花山下
永陵	朱厚熜	嘉靖	世宗	肃皇帝	1521—1566	宪宗孙	60	北京昌平区天寿山阳翠岭下
昭陵	朱载垕	隆庆	穆宗	庄皇帝	1566—1572	世宗三子	36	北京昌平区天寿山大峪山下
定陵	朱翊钧	万历	神宗	显皇帝	1572—1620	穆宗三子	58	北京昌平区天寿山大峪山下
庆陵	朱常洛	泰昌	光宗	贞皇帝	1620	神宗长子	39	北京昌平区天寿山黄山寺二岭下
德陵	朱由校	天启	熹宗	悊皇帝	1620—1627	光宗长子	23	北京昌平区天寿山潭峪岭下
思陵	朱由检	崇祯		庄烈愍皇帝	1627—1644	光宗五子	35	北京昌平区天寿山鹿马山下

摄影/张树林　Photography by Zhang Shulin

作者简介：

　　周元庆，中国摄影家协会会员，中国艺术摄影学会会员，北京摄影家协会会员，高级摄影技师；现于华北电网有限公司北京十三陵蓄能电厂任职。

Introduction to Photographer：

　　Zhou Yuanqing, senior photographer, a member of China Photographers Association, China Artistic Photography Association and Beijing Photographer Association, is currently working for Beijing Shisanling (Ming Tombs) Pumped Storage Power Plant of North China Grid Company Limited.

图片说明参考了胡汉生先生的著作，特致谢意。
Thanks to Mr. Hu Hansheng for referencing his book to my album.

明陵今照　　中石题
New Look of the Ming Tombs
Inscribed by Ouyang Zhongshi

摄影／文字　周元庆
Photographed/noted by Zhou Yuanqing

编委 The Edit members
回金方　　　Hui Jinfang
王维洁　　　Wang Weijie
任志武　　　Ren Zhiwu
姜桂德　　　Jiang Guide
赵宝永　　　Zhao Baoyong
张恒谦　　　Zhang Hengqian

设计　陈磊
Designed By Chen Lei
翻译　王维洁
Translated by Wang Weijie

图书在版编目（CIP）数据

明陵今照／周元庆摄. —北京：中国档案出版社，2007.5
ISBN 978-7-80166-826-4
Ⅰ.明… Ⅱ.周… Ⅲ.十三陵—摄影集 Ⅳ.K928.76-64
中国版本图书馆 CIP 数据核字(2007)第 048310 号

出版／中国档案出版社(北京市宣武区永安路106号 100050)
发行／新华书店
印刷／北京鑫益晖印刷有限公司
规格／787×1092 印张／20
版次／2007年6月第1版 2007年6月第1次印刷

定价／360.00元